SO-BON-830

Discovering
NEWPORT
Rhode Island

A Visitor's Guide
to the City by the Sea

Discovering
NEWPORT
Rhode Island

Discovering Newport Rhode Island.
Copyright © 2015 Burt Jagolinzer. Produced and printed by Stillwater River Publications. All rights reserved. Written and produced in the United States of America. This book may not be reproduced or sold in any form without the expressed, written permission of the author and publisher.

Visit our website at **www.StillwaterPress.com** for more information.
First Stillwater River Publications Edition
ISBN-10: 0-692-48452-3
ISBN-13: 978-069248452-4
Library of Congress Control Number: 2015946354
1 2 3 4 5 6 7 8 9 10
Written by Burt Jagolinzer
Photographs by Steven R. Porter except where noted
Cover design by Dawn M. Porter
   Published by Stillwater River Publications, Glocester, RI, USA

INDEX

DISCOVERING NEWPORT

Newport was one of the first cities established in America (1639).

The city is located on Aquidneck Island in Narragansett Bay less than 25 miles south of Providence, Rhode Island. The island is 14.5 miles long and approximately 5 miles wide.

There are approximately 25,000 year round residents with the number nearly doubling during the tourist season.

Sightseeing is available by trolley, van, private vehicle, bike or moped rental.

Newport's Point Section has one of the largest groupings of original Colonial homes in America. The Colonial Era is considered to be 1600's and 1700's.

The historic cemetery on Farewell Street (established in 1636) is believed to be the only cemetery of that era where Africans are buried next to Caucasians including Jews, Catholics, Protestants, Baptists, Methodists, Presbyterians, Lutherans and Quakers.

Over 600 mansions were built in Newport after the American Civil War (late1800's). Wealthy summer visitors came to escape the oppressive heat of the industrial cities of New York, Philadelphia, and Boston. (There was no electricity, fans, or air-conditioning during this period.)

Some 550 mansions still remain from that era and are mostly found on the side streets of the city. Newport has always been known for its pleasant summer temperatures of 70-80 degrees, with a soft breeze.

Today a small group of mansions are open to the public. Most are presented by the Newport Preservation Society who can be reached at **(401) 847-1000.**

Cardine's Field is the old baseball stadium located downtown across from The Marriott Hotel. It is one of the oldest baseball parks in America. In the early days of the sport there was no "spring training," so major league teams would travel from city to city creating their own training. Many of the sport's greatest players played here, including Babe Ruth, Honus Wagner, Ty Cobb, Tris Speaker and John McGraw.

Today the Newport Gulls play throughout the summer in the well-organized New England Collegiate Baseball League (NECBL).

While walking along Newport's famous Thames Street or America's Cup Boulevard, you'll find a small park that leads up to a hill where the old Trinity Church shines beautifully in the distance. The church was built in 1789 by London's world famous architect, Sir Christopher Wren. It is the oldest Episcopal

construction in Rhode Island. (Earlier Episcopal churches were built in Boston). Even
George Washington prayed here in a special
pew. Tours are available. **(401) 846-0660.**

Newport's only appreciable hill connects the
beaches and other important areas via Memorial Drive which begins at the base of the hill
at Thames Street.

One block up the hill on the right is St. Mary's
Roman Catholic Church built in1828. It is the
oldest Catholic Church in Rhode Island and
one of the oldest in America. On September 12,
1953, Jacqueline Bouvier married John F. Ken-
nedy, who in 1957, would become the 35th

President of the United States. Their wedding reception took place three miles away from this church at Hammersmith Farm, the home of Jacqueline's mother and stepfather, where she had spent a good portion of her early life.

At the top of Memorial Drive (on your right, on Bellevue Avenue) is one of the oldest shopping centers in the country. It was built in the late 1800's to give the summer's wealthy women a place to shop. Initially, the mall was stocked with branches of New York stores, offering only the finest clothing available. No money was ever exchanged, but signed invoices were sent to their permanent estates in Philadelphia, Boston and New York to collect payment.

In the middle of this shopping center, one of the earliest tennis clubs in America was built. It was purposely constructed to resemble the facilities at London's Wimbledon. Today it is the home of the International Tennis Hall of Fame and Museum which is open for tours. **(401) 849-3990.** The first Newport Jazz Festival took place here in 1954.

At this important intersection (facing the shopping center) you can travel in one of three additional directions.

To the left (on Bellevue Avenue) you will find the famed Newport Art Museum, which is on your right side and the famous Redwood Library, the oldest known lending library in the United States which opened in 1747. On the other side of the street you will find the Elks Club Mansion, which was the home of the U.S. Naval Academy during the Civil War.

Behind the mansion is the Channing Memorial Universalist Church at 135 Pelham Street, the first Universalist Church in the world founded in 1835 by William Ellery Channing (grandson to the signer of the Declaration of Independence) who was eager to begin a new religion of his own. His statue is located directly across from the church's entrance. **(401) 846-0643.**

In the park behind his statue stands the famous Stone Mill which many believe to have been built by Viking explorers possibly as early as 1600. Others question the theory.

Back on Bellevue Avenue on the left is the famous Viking Hotel believed to be Newport's first major hotel, established by wealthy Newport families to house their growing list of summer visitors.

Further down Bellevue Avenue you will find The Touro Synagogue & Visitors Bureau on the right. Touro Synagogue was built in 1658 and is America's first synagogue. George Washington, who visited here sent a now famous and important letter on the importance of religious liberty, stating, *"that this country would not sanction bigotry..."* Tours are available. **(401) 847-4794.**

At 49 Division Street (across from Touro Synagogue) you will also find the First Free Black Church in America established here in 1783.

Within walking distance from here, you can also visit the First Congregational Church (1695) and St. Peters Lutheran Church (1892). And in another short walk, you will see the First Baptist Church (1644), First

Quaker Meeting House (1699) and St. Paul's Methodist Church (1800). On nearby Broadway, at the corner of Everett Street, you will also find the First Presbyterian Church (1892).

Note: All these "first" churches are within walking distance of one another, and the different congregations all got along quite well in the early days. It is a shining example of America's original way of life and stood as a model for the future design for our nation.

In the center of Washington Square (named after General George Washington who was a regular visitor to Newport) is the Colony House (1741) where many important early political meetings and local events took place. The Colony House served as the State Capital of Rhode Island until 1900 when the Capital was moved permanently to Providence.

Several blocks up Broadway (on your right) at the corner of Stone Street is the Wanton-Lyman-Hazard House, the oldest in Rhode Island and one of the oldest in America. It is now a museum-house, operated by the Newport Historical Society. **(401) 846-3622.**

Just outside Washington Square (on Marlborough Street) is the famous White Horse Tavern (1673), oldest continually operating tavern in the nation where important politicians and the like continue to imbibe even today. **(401) 849-3600.**

Back on Memorial Boulevard (at the top of the hill) going past the shopping center takes you further down Bellevue Avenue passing by many of the finest mansions. The side streets are loaded with other spectacular mansions, as well as the campus of Salve Regina University.

At the end of Bellevue Avenue begins the famous ten mile Ocean Drive, featuring exclusive homes and breathtaking scenery along

the Atlantic Ocean waterfront. Some consider it to be the best example of the Italian Riviera on the North American continent.

Back at the top of Memorial Boulevard's hill you can continue down to First Beach (Easton's Beach). Just before that beach, on the right, is the beginning of the 3.5 mile long Cliff Walk. The Cliff Walk is a free walking path that snakes its way along the Atlantic Ocean and passes by many of the front yards that still belong to Newport's wealthiest summer residents. Good walking shoes are highly recommended.

First Beach is a very general and popular public beach along the Atlantic seaboard, with moderate waves. There is no charge, except for parking.

Traveling straight ahead and up the next hill into the township of Middletown, you will see St. George's Prep School on your left.

Travel a little farther and you will come upon Second Beach which boasts larger waves and sand dunes. This is also a free public beach, with paid parking available. It is a great beach for surfing and getting knocked down by the waves. It is the most popular of the area's three public beaches.

If you keep travelling past Second Beach, you will come to Third Beach. This too is a free public beach, except for parking. This beach is more of an inlet, is quite calm and is wonderful for swimming.

This great availability of quality public beaches is very unusual along the Eastern Seaboard of America.

COLONIAL ERA
THE POINT SECTION

Some 200 Colonial-era homes grace The Point Section of Newport. These homes were built in the 1600's, 1700's and some in the early 1800's.

The homes were constructed mostly out of timber harvested from the heavily-wooded Newport and surrounding areas. Some were built with available rock and stone taken from the ground, left behind by glaciers from the great ice age that had swept through this portion of the country. The stone needed to be cleared from the ground so that early settlers could grow crops.

The Point Section is one of the oldest parts of Newport, having been first settled circa 1639.

You will note how these homes were closely built to one another, helping to cut down the wind, thus offering a warmer winter. Also, by being close together, they benefitted from the added security, deterring others who might think to harm them.

Most of these edifices are historically valuable. Their current real estate worth is quite high, based upon condition and location. Their closeness to Newport's downtown increases their desirability.

Many of these special homes have been passed down from generation to generation to generation. Some original names still draw historical attraction in the community.

CONVENTION & VISITORS BUREAU

The Newport Convention & Visitors Bureau (The Gateway Center) is an important non-profit organization designed to promote the city and its five townships for business and tourism. It is strategically located downtown next to the Marriott Hotel and across from Cardine's Field.

Featured is a tour center where you can receive free information, literature and purchase tickets to many Newport attractions. Free parking is available on site.

This organization aids in advertising and directing trade shows and sundry marketing efforts. **(401) 849-8048.**

CHAMBER OF COMMERCE

The Newport County Chamber of Commerce membership is very active in its support of city events, seminars and holiday programming.

The Chamber offers newsletters, special training, business interplay and family activities. **(401) 847-1600**.

STATISTICS

The City of Newport is the central focus of Newport County. The total island consists of the City of Newport and the townships of Middletown and Portsmouth.

Portsmouth (the oldest of the three) in the northern part of the island was founded in 1638 by early settlers. Some of them broke away and came south to establish the City of Newport (1639), and the land between the two became known as Middletown (1731).All three are on the island of Aquidneck.

Dr. John Clarke is credited with helping found Newport. After living several years in England, he obtained a written decree stating that the State of Rhode Island would be the first haven of religious freedom in America.

The original document is formally on display in the Capital at the State House in Providence.

NEED TO KNOW

Noise tolerance is very low in Newport. Police will stop and arrest violators of the tolerance levels. Check with the Newport Police for specific regulations.

An increase in late evening activities have caused security and local police to tighten enforcement of alcohol tolerance levels.

It is advised to have "designated drivers" at the wheel of all vehicles.

Parking regulations are strictly enforced on all main and side streets throughout the city. Towing is regularly instituted.

Cans or bottles containing alcohol, or any identifying cups may not be carried in the city.

Pedestrians in proper walkways have the "right-of-the-road" at crossings throughout the State of Rhode Island.

Trash cans are available most everywhere. You are expected to use them. Fines for littering are regularly enforced.

Speed limits are closely monitored by police and justly enforced.

RESTAURANTS

Newport boasts a wide variety of world class cuisine. Seafood and other local favorites top all the best menus. Native lobster, clams, assorted fish and homemade chowders capture the scene. Summer months (July, August and September) will also feature locally-grown butter & sugar sweet corn. Lemonade and coffee drinks are available everywhere.

Upscale restaurants include home cooking and specially prepared meats and vegetables. Restaurants vary in location, ambiance, and pricing. Usually, you will get the extras that you pay for. Sport dress is desirable.

Inexpensive restaurants tend to show their prices up front. They are nicely scattered throughout the city and can offer some great experiences.

Ethnic eating establishments usually require reservations during the evening. Newport features top Irish, Portuguese, French, Arabic, Greek and Italian food throughout the city. Excellent traditional American food is easily available, too. Pizza shops are most everywhere.

Credit cards are generally accepted at most locations.

Though casual dress is accepted throughout most of Newport, some formal restaurants appreciate better attire.

Newport's top restaurants: The Inn at Castle Hill, 22-Bowen's Wharf, Sardella's Restaurant, Momma Luisa's, The Canfield House, The Pier, Ocean Cliff, Vanderbilt-Grace, The Marriott Hotel, White Horse Tavern, The Black Pearl, The Barking Crab, The Chanler, The Clarke-Cooke House, Hotel Viking, The Hyatt-Regency

Hotel, 41-North, and The Newport Harbor Hotel & Marina.

Restaurants that feature top seafood dishes include Anthony's Seafood, The Mooring, The Brick Alley Pub, Flo's Clam Shack, La Forge Restaurant, The Lobster Bar and Rhea's Restaurant.

Other more informal establishments are available most everywhere. Luncheon diners and fast-food choices are found throughout the island.

TOURING THE CITY

Many people drive to the city searching for special interests. Driving is often congested in downtown and along Bellevue Avenue.

Parking can be a problem, too. Most event locations try their best to accommodate vehicles, but it can be quite challenging at times.

Hotels and bed & breakfasts can usually direct you to tour operators. The Convention and Visitors Center offers a sundry collection of tours, some with packages (**401) 849-8048**. Other tour companies will pick up at many other locations, most by reservation only.

Some tour companies will take you to the beaches and Ocean Drive. Still others focus on the mansions alone. Checking with tour operators prior to purchasing tickets on exactly what they will cover during their tour is recommended.

Private tours are usually available with a reservation. This could include private tour cars, taxis, sedans, trolleys and even buses.

Obviously the cost of private accommodations can differ and should be planned well in advance.

During high season (end of May through October) taxi service can be difficult to find. There are a limited number of taxis available on the island because Newport is basically a seasonal market. Other transportation can often help getting you to your destination.

BEACHES

First Beach (Easton's Beach) is located just down from the corner of Memorial Drive and Bellevue Avenue.

It boasts fine beach public facilities offering rental rooms for daily changing. The rooms can be rented for a week, month or the whole summer and include showers and rest rooms. On their boardwalk you will find lunch and plenty of places to eat your food.

The beach features a great carousal ride for the kids (and adults) and other amenities for children.

Second Beach (Sachuest Beach) is located straight ahead from First Beach and up over the hill. This public beach stretches nearly a mile with sand dunes and large waves that will knock you down if you aren't careful. It is great for surfing and it has become the young people's favorite beach.

At the end of Second Beach you will find signs leading to Third Beach, and it is a completely different from the other two. The water here is mostly calm, buoyant and wonderful for swimming. It is usually quiet with easy access and departure. This beach features a kayak rack, moorings and a boat ramp.

Several private beaches are also found along the ten mile Ocean Drive.

THE CLIFF WALK

One of the city's most popular attractions is to the famed Cliff Walk.

The free, non-profit walkway is maintained by the City of Newport. The Cliff Walk starts at the Memorial Boulevard entrance (next to First Beach) and continues for 3.5 miles along the spectacular Atlantic Ocean front, passing by many of Newport most elite mansions and summer cottages built during the late 1800's.

I recommend dressing for the weather, as well as bringing some water, sun screen, a hat, a camera and your best walking shoes.

Due to past hurricanes, weather conditions and erosion, some parts of the pathway change along the walk, making bikes and strollers unmanageable.

About a half-mile along the Walk you will come upon The Forty-Steps. Constructed in the 1800's for some local families to ease access to the ocean, it was originally built in wood but refurbished two decades ago with cement and stone.

In the early days, The Cliff Walk became a gathering place for parties and dances. Many a romance has begun here. Fishing and swimming often take place here, too, but it is at your own risk and not recommended. It is always a great setting for picture-taking.

Among the large mansions to see on the walk are Ochre Court (now an important part of Salve Regina University), The Breakers, Rose-cliff, Mrs. Astor's Beech House, Marble House and The Doris Duke Estate.

WARNING: Be prepared to return the same way you arrived -- there are no prudent short cuts for returning quickly.

The walkway was originally a Native American dirt path that circumvented the entire island. It became a common right-of-way.

When the wealthy "summer cottages" were built in the late 1800's they improved the walkway and shared it with each other, as a popular place to stroll. High Society referred to it as "an eloquent activity of the day."

LOCAL WINERIES

Newport has two excellent wineries.

Newport Vineyards is situated in the Middletown section of the island just a couple of miles north of downtown at 909 East Main Road. **(401) 848-5161**. It is owned by the Nunes family. They offer daily wine tasting. Weekend tasting requires reservations.

The other winery is just a few blocks further north on East Main Road in Portsmouth (just look for the signs). Here, Nancy and Bill Wilson operate Greenvale Vineyards **(401) 847-3777** at 582 Wapping Road, offering daily wine tasting as well. Reservations are recommended.

Both these establishments are available for private functions, parties and weddings. Just give them a call to determine availability.

THE MANSIONS

The non-profit Newport Preservation Society maintains many of the finest mansions in all Newport.

And they graciously open the doors to a number of their buildings charging minimal entrance fees that help in the upkeep of these historic buildings.

Reservations and ticket information can be obtained at **(401) 847-1000.**

Newport Preservation Society Properties

The Breakers: The largest mansion in Newport (1890). The CorneliusVanderbilt family mansion.

Chateau-sur-Mer: Classic Gilded Age mansion.

Chepstow: 19th Century period mansion.

The Elms: Early 20th Century mansion.

Hunter House: 18th Century period house.

Isaac Bell House: 1880's shingle-style mansion.

Kingscote: 19th Century Gothic Revival mansion.

The Marble House: Gilded Age William Vanderbilt family mansion.

Rosecliff: Gilded Age mansion modeled after the Grand Trianon in France.

Some Other Notable Mansions

Vernon Court: Home of National Museum of American Illustrations. Open for tours, **(401) 851-8949.**

Rough Point: The estate of the late Doris Duke, open for tours, **(401) 849-7300.**

Mrs. Astor's Beechwood: Under Renovation.

Belcourt Castle: Under new ownership.

Edward King House: The Newport Senior Center **(401) 846-7426**.

Clarendon Court: Currently for sale.

Ochre Court: Part of the Salve Regina University campus, **(800) 637-0002.**

MUSEUMS

Mrs. Astor's Beechwood Art Museum: Featuring an 18th and 19th Century art collection.

Fort Adams Park & Museum: Late 1800's U.S. Army fortification overlooking Narragansett Bay.

International Tennis Hall of Fame and Museum: Learn about the complete history of tennis. Tournaments.

Museum of Newport History: Located on Thames Street in, downtown Newport.

Museum of Yachting: Enjoy a history of sailing and yachting at this museum located next to Fort Adams.

National Museum of American Illustration: A collection of illustrated art is on display in this classic Gilded Age mansion (Vernon Court).

U.S. Naval War College Museum: A complete history of naval warfare.

Newport Art Museum: Features notable works from many Rhode Island and New England artists.

The Norman Bird Sanctuary and Museum

Touro Synagogue and Museum

Whitehall Museum: An 18th Century period house.

TEN-MILE OCEAN DRIVE

Newport's popular ten mile ocean drive begins at the end of Bellevue Avenue. It meanders along the Atlantic seacoast displaying all the beauty Southern New England has to offer.

Castles and mansions dart the landscape with spectacular marine settings to highlight the drive. Private swim clubs and the Newport Country Club are nestled in along the route.

There are also excellent opportunities for ocean fishing from choice rock areas on the route.

Along the way, you will pass Brenton Point State Park where the winds and the clear sky setting make it one of the world's finest kite-flying locations. Local, regional, national and international events take place here through-out the summer.

The park is also an excellent picnic area, vis-ited by tourists and locals alike who arrive by bicycle, scooter, trailer or on foot.

ANNUAL EVENTS

St. Patrick's Day Parade (March)

Newport Police Parade (early May)

Annual Chowder Festival (early June)

Newport Charter Yacht Show (June)

Annual Newport Flower Show (June)

Fourth of July Fireworks (July)

Annual Newport Music Festival (July)

Black Ship Festival (July)

Newport Folk Festival (end of July)

Newport Jazz Festival (early August)

VJ-Day Celebrations (August)
(World War II, victory over Japan)

Annual Greek Food Festival (September)

Annual Newport International Boat Show (September) Several Sailing & Boating Events (TBA)

Christmas in Newport (December)

CHILDREN'S ACTIVITIES

Most children enjoy boat rides. Newport offers sailing, charter excursions, and private boat experiences.

Ryan's Game Center on Thames Street offers ice cream, arcade games and candy galore.

There is a carousel ride at First Beach, horse rentals at nearby Middletown and plenty of surfing at Second Beach.

Biking & Moped Rentals: There are several biking and moped rental companies in downtown Newport. Usually you can rent for a few hours, a day, a weekend or even the season.

CAUTION: The State of Rhode Island expects you to obey all the rules and give courtesy to pedestrians throughout the city.

HOTELS AND BED & BREAKFASTS

Newport has only a limited group of major hotels. Included are The Marriott, The Chanler, Hyatt-Regency, Vanderbilt-Grace, The Inn at Castle Hill, OceanCliff, Newport Bay Club, Wyndham Properties, Newport Harbor & Marina, 41-North and The Hotel Viking.

They are all fully equipped to give you most of the amenities required. During the "season" reservations are a must. Some hotels insist on several-night stays only.

Rates will differ according to dates and needs.

Newport is believed to have the second largest number of bed and breakfasts in North America. San Francisco is believed to be first.

Among the more than 100 bed and breakfasts in Newport, rates can range from $75 per night to many hundreds depending on location, numbers of people, and scale of amenities. Dining opportunities can vary as well. Once again, reservations in advance are usually required.

Other Accommodations

Newport also has a few rooming houses, a marine hostel and boat charters that can sleep individuals. Weekly, monthly or seasonal rentals are available through real-estate establishments.

Many of the major hotels and some bed' n breakfasts can accommodate guests with disabilities. It is recommended to call the Chamber of Commerce **(401) 847-1600** or Convention & Visitor Center **(401) 367-0013** for more information.

TENNIS

Rental of the courts at the International Tennis Hall of Fame are strictly by reservation only. **(401) 849-3990.**

Tennis courts for public are available throughout the island. Private swim clubs, beach clubs and some hotels offer available time on their private courts.

The universities and private schools have tennis facilities as well. Reservations are recommended.

UNITED STATES NAVAL BASE

The U.S. Naval Base in Newport is home to The United States Naval War College and Justice School.

The War College offers a ten month curriculum of study in war history and statistics.

Graduates and students of the College include top ranking military officers and leaders from around the world including Alan Shepard, commander of the Apollo 14 mission.

This base includes a War Museum that, at times, will be open to the public. The Officer's Club is also often opened for local civic and military activities.

Entrance to the base at Gate 1 requires permission and inspection. **(401) 841-4052**.

THE NEWPORT GULLS BASEBALL TEAM

The Gulls begin their scheduled season in June. Their home games are played at Cardine's Field across from the Marriott Hotel in downtown Newport.

The Gulls play teams from New Bedford (Massachusetts), Plymouth (Massachusetts), Providence (Rhode Island), Mystic (Connecticut) and Danbury (Connecticut) in the New England Collegiate Baseball League (NECBL).

The Gulls won the NECBL League Championship in 2014. It was their sixth time.

Tickets are available at the field or by telephone **(401) 845-6832.**

NEWPORT BY NIGHT

The summer evenings in Newport will often cool down to the 50's and 60's. Many find a light jacket to be useful.

Downtown is graced with an abundant number of pubs and restaurants that keep their doors open until the local curfew at 1 a.m.

Socialites and visitors enjoy working their way around town throughout the course of the evening. Music will be found most everywhere, both recorded and live.

The musical talent differs throughout the season and the local newspapers are usually the best way to find your element.

Other suburban areas offer some of the same.

A ride down upper Bellevue Avenue at night is a wonderful experience. The large mansions and their surroundings are lit to resemble the late 1800's. You can even picture horse-drawn carriages running up and down Bellevue Avenue from that special era.

The public beaches hold their beauty and romance during the late hours and are regularly visited by walkers and even late-night swimmers.

Scheduled evening events and activities are usually posted in newspapers and local hotels.

MUSIC

The annual Newport Music Festival, usually held in July, is one of the finest classical music events in the world. It includes performances from well-known veteran performers and newly discovered talents from around the globe.

Their works are presented in the mansions of the Newport Preservation Society and Salve Regina University.

These formal events are by reservation only, and tickets are limited. **(401) 846-1133.**

The world famous Newport Folk Festival takes place towards the end of July and is held at Fort Adams State Park.

The folk festival always includes top acts and new talent. The setting is on the lawn of the fort facing the Atlantic Ocean and beautiful Narragansett Bay. **(401) 848-5055.**

The renowned Newport Jazz Festival takes place usually around the beginning of August, at Fort Adams State Park. It's opening night usually takes place at the Casino, on Bellevue Avenue.

The jazz festival includes jazz's current veterans and new talent throughout a long weekend. Information **(401) 848-5055.**

The Newport Blues Café downtown on Thames Street offers headliners throughout the season. For reservations and information, call (401) 841-5510.

Local jazz performances can usually be found at Greenvale Winery, 582 Wapping Road in Portsmouth, on Saturday afternoons from 1 to 4 p.m. **(401) 847-3777.**

Other jazz performances take place at The Chanler Hotel on Friday evenings from September through April from 6 to 10 p.m. Still other jazz events are scheduled throughout the year at The Hotel Viking, LaForge Restaurant and The Rum Line.

Rock, pop, fusion, rap, new music, and other styles can be found scattered around downtown particularly on weekends.

SAILING & SERVICES

Because of Newport's ideal location where a constant wind exists, it is called "the sailing capital of the world." Many veteran sailors consider Newport to be a sailor's dream.

The harbors are generally loaded with sail craft all year long.

Local Services

Sail Newport: sailing lessons and rentals of all sizes. **(401) 846-7245**.

Classic Cruises (including Rum Runner II): **(401) 847-0298**.

SightSailing: **(401) 849-3333**.

The Adirondack Sailing Yacht, for charter **(401) 217-0044**.

FORT ADAMS STATE PARK

The fort was built in 1840 as a large seacoast fortification for the United States Army in the defense of Southern New England. It was named in honor of our second president, John Adams.

Fortunately, it was never put to wartime use.

In the late 20th Century, the federal government decided to give the large parcel to the State of Rhode Island to use for recreational programs.

The fort offers daily tours.

Portions of the land are used for picnics, boating and scenic pleasure. The Newport Folk and Jazz Festivals take place here every summer. The Newport Yachting Museum also has its home here.

Other seasonal activities are performed on site. **(401) 841-0707.**

THEATERS

There are several movie theaters located on the island.

The historic Jane Pickens Theatre built in 1834 features special films and performances. **(401) 846-5474.**

The Newport Playhouse & Cabaret Restaurant offers a variety of live plays with an optional dinner combination. **(401) 848-7529.**

Newport Murder Mystery (at The Newport Art Museum). **(401) 324-9436**

The Opera House, built in 1867, is currently under new management.

FISHING

Charter boats are generally available at dockside downtown for deep sea fishing. Some specialize in day trips and fish for flounder, scup, sea bass, mackerel and sea perch.

Others fish for striped bass, cod and even tuna. Reservations are a must.

Fishing from the beaches, rocks and docks in the area sometimes will catch you big fish and lots of smaller ones. Local bait stores provide rentals, bait and good information about suitable locations.

KITE FLYING

Possibly the best kite flying spot in the world exists at Brenton Point State Park. The wind and clear ceiling are always available in this setting.

Local and world events take place here throughout the summer, but there is always room for family flyers. Homemade kites will often be seen flying here.

Local kite stores can be found in downtown Newport for both rental and purchases.

SHOPPING

Shopping in Newport is world class and includes original art, assorted crafts, some national stores, local boutiques, galleries and souvenir stores. Most are located along Thames Street, Broadway and America's Cup Boulevard.

And many antique shops are located on Franklin Street, just off Thames Street.

POST OFFICE

Newport's main post office is located at the corner of Thames and Franklin Streets.

There is a second, smaller office on Broadway several blocks from the downtown area.

Postal boxes can be found at key locations throughout the city.

GOVERNMENT

The City of Newport is headquartered at City Hall (43 Broadway) just a short distance from downtown Newport.

The city is governed by a mayor, three city councilors and three at-large councilors. A city manager is employed to run the program.

ARCHITECTURE

Newport features one of the most diverse mix of architecture in America.

Though a small city, it displays original edifices of early American workmanship from the 1600's right through modern examples in 21st Century. Side streets are full of examples of varied periods of architectural accomplishments, many built by immigrants whose quality of skills were put to use here in Newport.

The interiors of many of these side-street wooden homes exhibit master workmanship that money couldn't buy today.

The city has been blessed with magnificent edifices built, designed or created by some of the world's finest and famous architects. They include work by Sir Christopher Wren, Richard Morris Hunt, Peter Harrison, George Champlin Mason, H.H. Richardson and many others.

Their work can be found in spectacular mansions, private buildings and other structures throughout the city.

SCHOOLS

The island has an excellent public school system boasting highly educated students from elementary, middle schools and three nationally-recognized high schools.

These public schools are supplemented by an interesting selection of private schools as well as three colleges.

Salve Regina University is a co-educational arts and sciences school offering graduate and undergraduate studies in several areas. Founded in 1946, it has been under the leadership of Roman Catholic Sisters of Mercy.

The Community College of Rhode Island (CCRI) has a beautiful new campus in Newport. It offers general education opportunities for many on the island's students.

The U.S Naval War College (established in 1884) continues to draw military individuals from around the world to its campus and offers a ten month program in war history. The college is situated on The Newport Naval Base located next to the downtown area of Newport.

Also at the Navy Base is the Naval Justice School and one of the U.S. Navy's Officer Candidate Training Schools (OCS).

The Yacht Restoration School on Lower Thames Street, on the Waterfront, teaches individuals the art of wood-boat restoration. They renovate old shop-worn vessels that are sometimes donated. Others are purchased.

Master restoration takes place by students and instructors. The school is recognized world-wide for their workmanship and belief in the protection the historical integrity of old marine wooden sailing vessels.

PORT OF CALL

Because of Newport's unique location along the Atlantic seaboard, and its deep ocean port, it has always been an attractive stop for cruise ships.

The U.S. Navy also attracts large visiting vessels on occasion from around the world to its deep water docks.

Newport's varied social attractions make a day in the city desirous for chartered ships as well.

For decades, Newport has been considered one of the finest ports along the eastern Atlantic coast.

NEARBY ACTIVITIES

Many of the following activities require planning and special directions.

Gambling

- Newport Grand - Newport
- Twin River Casino - Lincoln, RI (40 minutes)
- Foxwoods Casino - Mashantucket, CT (1 hr.)
- Mohegan Sun Casino - Uncas, CT (1.5 hrs.)

Providence Activities

Waterfire, Brown University, Rhode Island State Capital, Providence Place Mall, Roger Williams State Park & National Memorial.

Other

- Battleship Cove (featuring the U.S.S. Massachusetts) - Fall River, MA (30 minutes)
- The Gilbert Stuart Art Museum - North Kingstown, RI (30 minutes)
- The University of Rhode Island - Kingston, RI (30 minutes)
- Roger Williams University - Bristol, RI (30 minutes)
- Cape Cod (1.5 hrs.)
- Boston (1.5 hrs.)
- New York City (4 hrs.)
- Antiquing, flea-markets and yard sale opportunities are numerous and will be found listed in local newspapers.

EMERGENCY CARE

The Newport Hospital is centrally located, just off Broadway about a mile from downtown center. **(401) 846-6400.**

It is a regional center for most injuries and up-to-date medical care. It boosts excellent physicians and administrators with a 24-hour emergency facility attached to the main hospital.

Other local private aid is available, including resident specialists who maintain offices across the island.

Ambulance and fire rescue vehicles keep 24-hour alert. **(401) 845-5900.**

Veteran's emergency services are available through U.S. Naval Station. **(401) 841-3456.**

TRAVEL AND TRANSPORTATION

At the Newport Convention & Visitor's Center (next to the Marriott Hotel and across from Cardine's Field) you'll find the bus terminal with transportation to Providence, Fall River, Boston and elsewhere. They provide connections to other buses to New York City, Cape Cod and most of the country.

Train services are available from either Kingston (45 minutes away) or Providence (1.5 hours away). From there you can connect to Boston, New York and other destinations. Schedules vary and reservations are suggested.

Local taxis and transportation companies can accommodate distant pick-ups and departures with reservations.

MONEY / ATM

The city of Newport features several major banks and their ATM's are located all over the island. Some stores, fuel stations and restaurants also have ATM's on the premises. The downtown Newport area has displayed several key ATM's for your convenience.

All major credit cards are accepted.

GOLF COURSES

There are many individual excellent golf courses within reach of Newport.

Each course is quite different, featuring narrow or wide fairways, various distances and numbers of holes. Prices for green fees also vary and you are encouraged to telephone for quotes and reservation times.

Jamestown Golf Course **(401) 423-9930**

Newport Country Club **(401) 846-9227**

Newport National Golf Club **(401) 846-1489**

Wanumetonomy Golf & Country Club **(401) 847-5141**

Green Valley Country Club **(401) 847-9543**

ABOUT THE AUTHOR

Burt Jagolinzer has been a registered tour guide in the City of Newport, Rhode Island for over twenty years. For thirteen of those years, he owned and operated his own tour company providing visitors, celebrities and guests with informative, personal in depth tours of the city.

Burt is the author of the music memoir *'Round Newport*, which chronicles his love of jazz and his personal visits to all 60 Newport Jazz Festivals.

22520233R00050

Made in the USA
Middletown, DE
04 August 2015